KidCaps' Presents
The History of the Civil War for Kids

KidCaps is An Imprint of BookCaps™

www.bookcaps.com

© 2012. All Rights Reserved.

Table of Contents

INTRODUCTION	5
CHAPTER 1: WHAT LED UP TO THE AMERICAN CIVIL WAR?	7
CHAPTER 2: WHY DID THE AMERICAN CIVIL WAR HAPPEN?	12
CHAPTER 3: WHAT HAPPENED DURING THE AMERICAN CIVIL WAR?	17
CHAPTER 4: WHAT WAS IT LIKE TO BE A KID DURING THE AMERICAN CIVIL WAR?	22
CHAPTER 5: HOW DID THE AMERICAN CIVIL WAR END?	24
CHAPTER 6: WHAT HAPPENED AFTER THE AMERICAN CIVIL WAR?	25
CONCLUSION	26
WORK CITED	27

About KidCaps

KidCaps is an imprint of BookCaps™ that is just for kids! Each month BookCaps will be releasing several books in this exciting imprint. Visit are website or like us on Facebook to see more!

Introduction

The men had been marching for days, it seemed. It was late June in the year 1863, and they had been fighting for a long time. These Union soldiers were serious men and they recognized how important it was for them to keep fighting this war. Even so, there were times when it wasn't easy. In their heavy blue uniforms made of dyed blue wool, they felt very hot. The sweat rolled down their foreheads and into their eyes, stinging them shut. Even though, it felt good to close their eyes for a moment against the bright June sun.

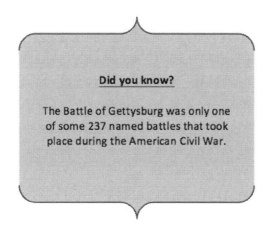

Did you know?

The Battle of Gettysburg was only one of some 237 named battles that took place during the American Civil War.

A young boy walked alongside the group and beat his little drum. The sound kept the soldiers marching together, moving closer and closer towards the little town that lay before them.

Gettysburg.

The soldiers had heard that there were some Confederate troops in the area, moving southwards towards them. A battle was going to happen, that much they could be sure of. In this war the battles kept coming and the men kept dying. What they didn't know, however, was that this battle, the Battle of Gettysburg, would become the best-known and most famous battle of the entire Civil War. Before it was over three days later, the fighting would leave more than 45,000 soldiers from both sides dead on the ground.

Smoke would fill the air, and the smell of burnt gunpowder and cannon shot would be everywhere. Men would scream as they charged the enemy, and they would scream again as they were shot by powerful guns. Horses would carry strong generals who commanded large armies, and the dead would be carried off by their friends to be buried. There would be acts of absolute heroism and brilliant strategy on both sides and, against the odds, both armies would have some amazing victories and some devastating losses.

During this time, large groups of soldiers (like the one we just saw) marched together towards Gettysburg. The Confederates came from the north and from the west and the Union troops from the south and the east. The soldiers marched on, listening to the beat of the boy with the drum, moving steadily towards the sleepy town ahead.

The Battle of Gettysburg was one of the most important moments of the Civil War. Have you ever heard of the American Civil War? Do you know what a civil war is? Unlike most wars, when one country fights against another country, a civil war is when a country fights against itself. Wars like these have happened in the history of almost every country, and they are always very tragic. Why so? Well, in a civil war, the soldiers are not fighting against strangers; they are fighting against people that they know. Sometimes, they have to meet friends, neighbors, schoolmates, and even family members on the battlefield. Can you imagine how hard it would be to fight against someone that you loved? No matter what the cause, civil wars are always very tragic for everyone involved.

You may wonder how the American Civil War got started. After all, America is the "land of the free", and different opinions and different lifestyles are allowed. So what could make different groups of Americans so upset that they would be willing to fight? What could have led up to a war like this?

In this handbook, we will be talking in detail about the causes of the American Civil War. What would you like to know about it? Well, we will be talking about some of the events that led up to this important war and what some of the main causes were. Then, we will look at some of the principal battles, technologies, and people that were involved in the war.

Do you think you would have liked to have been alive back then? If so, then get ready, because we will show you just what it would have been like to travel with a group of soldiers onto the battlefield. We will see how the American Civil War ended, and what happened afterward.

In this handbook, you will see lots of cool little boxes on the sides of the pages. Take a second to read them, because they will help you to better understand what America was like back then. They will also give you valuable information about the people, places, and things that formed part of the American Civil War.

> The American Civil War lasted from April 12, 1861 until May 9, 1865. Over 625,000 Americans died, and about 412,000 more were wounded.

Are you ready to learn more? Then let's start with what led up to the Civil War.

Chapter 1: What led up to the American Civil War?

Have you ever been mad at someone? Were you so angry that you were willing to hit that person, or to get into a fight with them? No matter how mad we get, we know that it is wrong to start a fight. It is better to talk about our problems or to get someone to help us to make peace with the other person. Well, back in the 1800s, the United States started to divide into two groups of people, and these two groups started to get mad at each other and they wanted to fight. Who were these two groups? This section is going to tell us about who these groups of people were. Although they started off as friends, they ended up being enemies. Let's find out how.

> **Did you know?**
>
> Almost half of the delegates to the Constitutional Convention in 1787 owned slaves.

To begin with, let's go back to the year 1787, the year that the United States Constitution was written. The group of men who prepared the constitution was from a wide variety of backgrounds: some were soldiers, others were farmers, some were inventors, and most were politicians. Although they had different ideas about what makes a country strong, they wanted to make sure that all Americans (and their opinions) would be protected under this new document which they were preparing. They wanted everyone to feel safe and happy in the United States. So, even though some of the men did not like slavery, they made sure that those who did have slaves would be happy in the new country as well. After all, slaves gave the states more votes and more taxes.

As the years went on, however, many states in the northern part of the country began to think that slavery was a really bad thing. What do you think? Is slavery a good idea or a bad idea? Is it right to buy a human like an animal and to make them work hard for long hours, all with no pay? A lot of people thought that it was bad. After the American Revolution, all of the Northern States had passed laws to ban slavery (the last one was New Jersey in 1804). The Northern states thought that slavery was a pretty bad thing.

The Constitution (written in 1787) had said that, after 1807, no more slaves could be brought into the country. The hopes of many Northerners were that, with the ban on supporting the international slave trade in place, slavery would simply die out. However, did that happen? Not at all, and for one main reason: the invention of the cotton gin.

Do you what a cotton gin is? Have a look at the picture on the right and you will see one. This little machine let farmers clean the sticky seeds out of balls of cotton faster than ever before.

Because the machine worked so well, the farmers made a lot of money (and wanted to make even more). As a result, when 1807 came around, the Southern farmers had no intention of letting slavery die out; they wanted it to grow more and more.

As the United States continued to grow in size, the two groups became more and more divided. For example, there was a large piece of territory acquired by President Jefferson in 1803, called the Louisiana Purchase. This large area of land was soon divided up into territories and states. However, with the new land came new questions: would the new territories and states be allowed to have slaves or not? The Northern states thought that the new land should not have slaves; the Southern states thought that they should. Motivated by different reasons, Americans were starting to find themselves agreeing with one or the other of these two very different groups.

After the Mexican-American War (which lasted from 1846 to 1848) the U.S. government acquired even more territory. The Southern slave states started making more noise than ever and demanded that these new lands be allowed to have slaves. What would the government do to make everyone happy?

In 1850, a series of bills (decisions by the government) were approved in order to keep a fight from breaking out. Together, these bills were called the Great Compromise of 1850. Two of them made Southerners very happy: new territories could decide for themselves whether or not they wanted to allow slavery, and the Northern states would be forced to support the Fugitive Slave Act. What was this act all about?

When slavery was allowed in the South, some slaves would do their best to escape to the free North, or even all the way to Canada. For years, there were people who worked together to help runaway slaves. The route that these slaves took, from one house to the next, was called the "underground railroad". Southern slave owners were furious that Northerners were helping runaway slaves. The new law *forced* all Northerners- especially police officers- to bring runaway slaves back to their owners. If they didn't, they could get in big trouble.

An important invention

The cotton gin allowed farmers to process and sell 50 times more cotton than before. They wanted to grow more cotton and they wanted more slaves to help them to do it.

However, even after the Great Compromise of 1850, the issue of slavery was still a big one. During his presidential campaign in the year 1860, candidate Abraham Lincoln had shown himself to be a moderate man focused on preserving the Union (the United States). The issue of slavery had separated the Democratic political party in two, so the Republican Party (represented by Lincoln) won an easy victory in November of 1860.

In his inaugural address, President Lincoln made it clear that he did not have any intention of interfering with slavery in the Southern states. However, he would not tolerate any attempts by them to leave the union, either. Note what he said during his speech:

> "It follows from these views that no State upon its own mere motion can lawfully get out of the Union; that resolves and ordinances to that effect are legally void, and that acts of violence within any State or States against the authority of the United States are insurrectionary or revolutionary, according to circumstances…I trust this will not be regarded as a menace, but only as the declared purpose of the Union that it will constitutionally defend and maintain itself… Plainly the central idea of secession is the essence of anarchy."

Knowing that Lincoln was a Republican and that he was born and raised in the North, the Southern states felt that action had to be taken. They felt that the Federal government simply wasn't listening to them anymore, and that it never would.

On December 24, 1860 (a little more than one month after Lincoln was elected) the state government of South Carolina adopted a very important document called the "Declaration of the Immediate Causes Which Induce and Justify the Secession of South Carolina from the Federal Union". Did you see the word "secession" in the document name? Do you know what it means?

To "secede" from the federal union was to "separate" or "leave" the Union. In other words, South Carolina no longer wanted to be a part of the United States.

Before Lincoln began serving as President in March of 1861, six more states (Mississippi, Florida, Alabama, Georgia, Louisiana, and Texas) had declared their independence from the Union. They formed a new country called The Confederate States of America. As part of this new country the Southerners elected a president (Jefferson Davis) wrote a constitution, and chose both a congress and a judicial branch.

Famous person

Abraham Lincoln was the Union President during the entire American Civil War.

When he became President, one of the first things that Lincoln did was to try and get back control of federal lands that were in Confederate territory. While he had no desire to fight a war against his fellow Americans, Lincoln felt that federal property had to be respected. As a result, military bases became the targets of southerners trying to kick the Northerners out of their territory.

Jefferson Davis was the Confederate President during the entire American Civil War

The first battle of the Civil War was fought at Fort Sumter, near Charleston in South Carolina. In April, Confederate cannons blasted away at the fort until it was finally forced to surrender on April 14, 1861.

One month after he took office, Lincoln had to decide how to react. He decided that he would stick with his original plan: get federal lands (including Fort Sumter) back under Union control. To do so, he asked for a volunteer army from the Northern states to help him go and get Fort Sumter back from the rebels.

When he did this, four more states (Virginia, Arkansas, North Carolina, and Tennessee) decided to leave the Union and to join the Confederate states of America. There were now eleven states fighting against the Union, and both sides wanted more military action.

One other contributing factor that led to the Civil War was the cultural difference between the two groups. Although they were all American, the South had focused much more on agriculture, while the North worked on developing its industry. The Southerners had their own culture, and they felt that they were not respected. As a result, many southerners, even soldiers and politicians, felt more loyalty to their Southern roots that they did to the U.S. government. When the war broke out, many of them joined the Confederate army to fight.

With those first shots fired at Fort Sumter and the call for more fighting, the American Civil War had begun.

Chapter 2: Why did the American Civil War happen?

The Civil War was one of the darkest times in American history. Almost one million people died or were wounded during the fighting, and everybody's lives- even those who were far away from the battlefield- were affected in one way or another. Although we understand some of the tensions that led up to the actual fighting, what finally pushed everyone over the edge? What were the three main causes of the Civil War? This section tells us everything we want to know.

Although there are lots of reasons why each soldier chose to pick up a gun and go out to that battlefield, there are three *main* reasons why the two groups (the Northern states and the Southern states) could not make peace and could not see eye to eye. What were they?

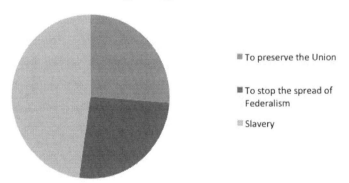

Let's look at each of these reasons one by one to understand more about why the Civil War was fought.

To preserve the Union. Do you remember President Lincoln's inaugural speech? He spoke a lot about "preserving the Union" and how the Union would "defend and maintain itself". What did he mean by those words? Well, when the United States was formed (first by the Articles of Confederation and later by the Constitution) it was only allowed because the majority agreed to do so. No state could be admitted to the Union unless a majority thought that it was a good idea and that it would make the country stronger. President Lincoln felt that the same should be true if a state decided to leave the Union. It should not be up to individual states to decide if they should stay or if they should go. Why not?

Did you know?
Although 11 states seceded from the Union, 25 states remained loyal to it.

Well, think about it this way: even though the goal of forming the United States was for the states to stand together against their enemies, each state also helped the others. For example, cotton from the South went to the North and was made into clothing and other important items. Machines and tools made in Northern factories helped Southern farmers to work more effectively and to have more comfortable homes. The states helped each other.

If all of the Southern states were to secede, then the whole country would suffer- including those living in the South. Enemies could attack both countries easier, and it would be harder to fight wars. However, there was another important reason to oppose the secession of the Southern states: it was illegal.

Did you know that the Constitution has laws for individuals, but also for state governments? It tells all American citizens, no matter who they are, what things are and are not allowed under law. For example, it is against the law for the government to stop another person from speaking their opinion- even if they don't like what the person is saying. The government also can't restrict what religion a person chooses to practice, as long as they aren't hurting anyone else. However, with all these freedoms, there are some things that a state or an individual cannot do. For example, although an individual can willingly give up his citizenship, a state government cannot. To do so would be an act of treason. Do you know what that word means?

Treason is when a person acts against the government where he lives. All those who seceded and fought against the Union, although they didn't see it like that, were committing treason according the laws of the United States. For that reason, Abraham Lincoln and the Northern army were convinced that the Union needed to be preserved for the good of the country and for all of its citizens.

To stop the spread of federalism. Do you know what the word "federalism" means? Well, it is related to the central United States government. "Federalism" talks about how much power the central government should have versus how much power the local state government should have. As time went on, the federal government began to take on more and more power and to make more decisions without talking to the states. A good example of this was the Louisiana Purchase. President Jefferson authorized the purchase without consulting Congress. Even though this turned out to be a good thing, decisions like that weren't always popular. For example, in 1820, the government agreed to the Missouri Compromise, which would make slavery illegal in all new states and territories (except Missouri) that were above the parallel 36°30′ north.

Many Southerners felt that the federal government did not have the right to determine who could and could not own slaves. Although they pointed to larger issues (the rights of the state to choose) the discussion was almost always about slavery (as we will see in a moment). The Southern states felt that the Federal government had gone too far and was making decisions that only the states should be making. For them, it was kind of like the principal of a school going to a student's house and telling him to clean his room and to eat his vegetables. Wouldn't it be strange for a principal to do that? After all, in the home it is the parents who are in charge, and the principal is in charge at school. For Southerners, they felt that "federalism" (the central government getting more and more power) was a bad thing for everybody.

Do you remember when we mentioned how the different cultures of the North and the South made a difference in how they saw things? Well, the Northerners didn't necessarily see a stronger central government as a bad thing; in fact, they kind of liked it. Remember, Southern Americans were farmers, and they felt that they were more self-reliant. They wanted a free market and no one to tell them what to do. Northern Americans relied more on factory jobs and technology, and they wanted protection from the state as they developed their industries more and more.

This difference of opinion made people want to either support more Federal power or to oppose it. What do you think: which side was right? It's not always easy to just draw a line in the sand and to take sides, but these two factors helped people to choose either loyalty to the Union or loyalty to the Confederacy.

> **Did you know?**
>
> In 1860, there were 3,950,511 slaves living in the United States!

In order to stop what they saw as an out of control government, and to protect their own interest and those of their state, eleven states and their citizens seceded from the Union and joined the Confederates.

Although the two reasons above were important, there is still an even more important one: slavery. Let's learn more.

Slavery. Slavery had been around since the early days of the American colonies. In the early 1700s, special sets of laws were prepared to tell everyone how slaves should be treated and what freedoms slave-owners had. Why were slaves so important to Southern Americans?

Northern Americans focused on crops that were primarily for their own use, or that could be grown without a lot of work. They grew grain, potatoes, corn, and other practical crops which weren't as hard to process as cotton was. In fact, cotton didn't grow very well at all in New England, so the Northerners didn't bother with it.

Southerners, on the other hand, focused most of their energies on growing cotton. Why? Well, cotton is what is called a "cash crop". What does that term mean? A "cash crop" is something that is grown just to make money. Unlike the crops that were grown in the North, which fed the farmers and other people, cotton was good only to sell. However, because it sold at high prices, Southern farmers wanted to grow more and more of it. With the invention of the cotton gin in 1793 (which we saw earlier) farmers could now grow and process larger amounts of cotton and make lots and lots of money. To do so, however, they needed more workers. They didn't want to pay money to anyone to work in their cotton fields, so they bought slaves to do all that hard work.

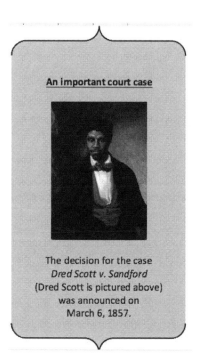

An important court case

The decision for the case
Dred Scott v. Sandford
(Dred Scott is pictured above)
was announced on
March 6, 1857.

As time went on, the North used slavery less and less, and the South used it more and more. With each new piece of land acquired by the government, Southern farmers thought of all the money that they could make there if they could just build a new farm and bring their slaves. What was the solution? Do you remember the Missouri Compromise that we mentioned earlier? In this decision by the government, it was decided that slavery would be illegal in all new states and territories (except Missouri) that were above the parallel 36°30′ north. Although this kept the peace for a while, things got heated up again when looking at the territories of Kansas and Nebraska. In 1854, the Kansas-Nebraska Act changed the laws and cancelled the Missouri Compromise. Instead of deciding geographically which states could have slaves, it was decided that each state would choose for itself whether or not to allow slavery. Called "popular sovereignty", the idea was to make both sides happy and to keep the government out of it.

However, large numbers of the two groups (those who liked slavery and those who did not) all moved to Kansas to influence the decision. They ended up fighting in the streets, and the territory came to be known as "Bleeding Kansas". It was like a preview of what would happen later during the Civil War.
During those years, Kansas, Missouri, and Texas were all admitted to the Union as slave states.

In 1857, the issue of slavery went all the way to the Supreme Court of the United States. The trial was about whether or not a slave could go to court against his master in order to get his freedom. This trial was about a slave named Dred Scott who had been with his owner for many years. This owner (who was a soldier) took Dred Scott with him into free territories (like Illinois and Wisconsin) and even let him marry a wife (something that only free persons could do). When his master died, Dred Scott tried to purchase his freedom from his master's widow, but she would not allow it. The case was eventually brought before the Supreme Court. What was their decision? Voting 7 to 2, the decision was that African-Americans brought into the United States as slaves were not American citizens and were not protected by the laws of the Constitution. Dred Scott remained a slave.

People across the nation had strong (and very different) reactions to the court case. Southerners cheered because it gave them the right to take their slaves with them anywhere, even into Free states. Northerners saw it as a push to allow slavery in the West, and worried about America's future. It was like pouring gasoline on a fire that was getting bigger and bigger every day. The country was completely divided over the issue of slavery.

Although there were various attempts at making peace, the fighting in Kansas showed that many Americans felt that the time for talk was over: they wanted to see action. One man, named John Brown, attacked a United States weapons warehouse on October 16, 1859, in order to start a slave revolt. He wanted to give weapons to all the slaves and to help them fight for their freedom. Although his efforts failed, he made the front page of every newspaper across the country and made people talk. As Abraham Lincoln said the next year when planning his presidential campaign:

> "This question of Slavery was more important than any other; indeed, so much more important has it become that no other national question can even get a hearing just at present."

According to President Lincoln, John Brown's raid on the weapons warehouse in the town of Harper's Ferry made slavery the most important issue of the time. Every politician had to talk about it in his speeches, and every citizen had to decide where they stood.

We already saw how seven states seceded from the Union and formed the Confederate States of America when Lincoln won the election. These states then attacked a Federal military base (Fort Sumter) and started to prepare for war. Four more states seceded when Lincoln raised an army to fight the rebels.

Although people talk about many causes when they speak about the Civil War, there can be no doubt: the primary cause of the Civil War was *slavery*.

Now that we understand what led up to the Civil War and why Americans were willing to fight in it, let's learn more about what actually happened during the Civil War.

Chapter 3: What happened during the American Civil War?

The American Civil War was a time of change in the United States. It was a time when friends and neighbors fought against each other and when the future of the entire country was uncertain. However, this war was also different than all other previous wars had been. There was new technology, different tactics, and large battles- a combination of things that had never before been seen in the Americas or even in the entire world. Let's look at some of the things that made the Civil War so unique. We will look at:

- **The unique tactics**
- **The famous battles**
- **The new technology**

The unique tactics. If you had to send armies to win a war, what kinds of tactics do you think you would use? Well, you might think that giving lots of men lots of guns would be enough. However, the generals who commanded the soldiers during the Civil War tried to think smarter than the other side. They tried to find soft spots in the other army and they even tried methods of making the other side weaker without killing them. Let's look at three interesting methods used by the Union armies to win the Civil War.

> **Did you know?**
>
> The Union commissioned about 500 ships to create a naval blockade that lasted from 1861 to 1865.

Economic warfare. Instead of just fighting on the battlefield, President Lincoln wanted to make the *all* of the Confederate states weaker economically. After all, if they didn't have any money, they couldn't fight in the war. One of the ways Lincoln made the South weaker economically was by creating a **naval blockade**. Do you know what a naval blockade is?

An important invention

The Confederacy printed their own money to help make them completely independent of the United States.

A naval blockade is when lots of ships surround the major ports of a country and do not allow anything to come in or to go out. Why was this naval blockade so effective? Well, do you remember what kind of agriculture the South focused on? That's right: they focused on cash crops, mainly cotton and tobacco. What do you think: can you eat cotton or tobacco? Of course not! Those crops are only good to be sold. Well, when the Union set up the naval blockade, no cotton or tobacco could be sold to Europe, and the North certainly wasn't going to buy any. As a result, the Southern economy (which depended on selling cotton and tobacco) collapsed.

Although the Confederacy had printed their own money, that money quickly became worthless. After all, the states weren't producing any income to support the value of that money. Soon, Confederate troops and their families back home ran low on food, clothing, and even weapons. If fact, some confederate soldiers marched into battle without any shoes on!

This economic situation was a complete surprise. A little while before the Civil War broke out the Southerners felt that they could do anything that they wanted because the whole world wanted their cotton. In one famous speech in the United States Senate, a Southern politician named James Henry Hammond expressed the confidence of the South when it comes to their cotton production:

> "But if there were no other reason why we should never have war, would any sane nation make war on cotton? Without firing a gun, without drawing a sword, should they make war on us we could bring the whole world to our feet… What would happen if no cotton was furnished for three years? I will not stop to depict what every one can imagine, but this is certain: England would topple headlong and carry the whole civilized world with her, save the South. No, you dare not make war on cotton. No power on earth dares to make war upon it. Cotton is king."

Did you understand why the South was so confident in their economic might? They thought that the world would do anything, even support their secession, to keep the supply of cotton coming. However, that is not at all what happened. In fact, it was just the opposite.

During the Civil War, the countries in Europe had their own problems. Instead of supporting the South (which the North had said would be an act of war) European countries worried about fighting their own wars. They got cotton from Egypt and from India, and preferred to buy Northern grain to feed their nations. With no cotton going out and no money or food coming in, the South began to have serious economic problems that would last beyond the war and into the next century.

The economic warfare of the North was an ingenious tactic, and it worked.

<u>Total war</u>. As the Civil War drew to a close, General Sherman of the Union army was told to go through the Southland and march all the way to the Atlantic Ocean. As he did so, he was to completely cripple the infrastructure (roads, bridges, train tracks, telegraph lines, etc…) that he found along the way. The idea was to make the South so weak that it could never again rise up and rebel against the Union. The tactic worked. The total war guaranteed that the South had no choice but to remain a part of the Union and to obey its laws.

<u>The Emancipation Proclamation</u>. Using his special wartime powers, President Abraham Lincoln issued the Emancipation Proclamation on January 1, 1863. What did this special proclamation say? Well, Lincoln's wartime powers suspended law in the rebelling states and allowed him to make special laws governing life there. The Emancipation Proclamation was such a law: it freed all slaves living in the rebelling states. Some 50,000 to 60,000 were freed immediately, and others were freed as the Union army advanced through the South. Why do we say that this was a smart wartime tactic?

This was a brilliant tactic because many of the freed slaves were eager to join the Union army and to fight against the Confederates. In a time when both sides were running low on new recruits, the Union got a boost of fresh soldiers who were motivated. After all, those men did not want to become slaves again, so they were willing to fight hard!

Famous battles. In a four-year long war with 237 named battles, there is no time to talk about all of the battles that were fought. We already spoke about the Battle of Gettysburg, which was the turning point, when the South began to retreat and to lose the war. However, another famous battle was the Battle of Antietam. What happened and why was it so important? Let's find out.

Did you know?

179,000 African-American soldiers fought in the Union Army

The Battle of Antietam (fought on September 17, 1862) was the first important battle of the Civil War that was fought on Union soil (in Maryland). About 23,000 Americans died that day, and it is still the bloodiest day of fighting in American history. It was part of the South's push northward that took place early in the war. It was thought that if the South could win a big battle like this one on Union soil, then other countries (like France and England) would be forced to take the rebels seriously and might even help them with money or weapons.

Although the fighting was fierce on each side, the Union army ended up winning and chasing the Confederacy back down to the South. This battle made sure that no foreign countries would step in to help the South.

Another historic battle took place on March 9, 1862. Do you remember how important the naval blockade was to Union strategy during the war? Well, the South tried as hard as they could to break that blockade and to fight against the many Union ships that were in the ocean. To do so, they covered a captured Union ship with iron plates and sailed it into the water. Called an "ironclad" this ship easily sunk two Union warships. The next day, a Union ironclad arrived, and the two fought for four hours, neither being able to sink the other. The battle ended when the Confederate ship slipped past the Union sailors and escaped into the night.

This battle was so important because it used new technology to fight a war. The ships were almost invincible, and they were the first step towards building the battleships and submarines of the future.

The new technology. Something that made the American Civil War more deadly than previous wars and more unique was its use of new technology. Unlike all the wars that had been fought before, usually with muskets and lines of marching soldiers, this war used technology to win the battles. The Northern soldiers especially, with the backing of the federal government, were the ones who received the best weapons, although the Southern soldiers worked hard to come up with new ideas. Let's look at a few of the technologies used for the first time during the Civil War: the better guns, the telegraph, and the submarine.

Better guns: The musket, the first popular type of gun, was used during the Revolutionary War and during the Civil War. The problem with muskets was that they weren't very accurate over long distances, and they took a while to load new bullets between shots. In Europe and the North, inventors and manufacturers got together to make better guns. The first big step was making bullets that were more accurate, and the second was making a gun that was easier to reload. Because only the North had the money to design and make them, they were the ones who got the better guns. The first gun to make a big impact was called the Spencer repeating rifle.

As a result of the more accurate guns that could fire over longer distances, troops began to dig trenches in order to protect themselves. This useful tactic would also be used later in World Wars I and II.

The telegraph: Do you know what a telegraph is? A telegraph was a way of communicating before telephones and radios were invented. They used electronic signals to transmit letters and words over electric lines. The telegraph (used mainly by the North) allowed President Lincoln and the commanding generals to receive instant reports about the battles and to give orders. Never before was such a thing possible, and it allowed the soldiers to react more quickly to changes on the battlefield.

The submarine: The first submarine in history that had a wartime victory was built by the Confederacy. Called the H. L. Hunley, it sunk a Union ship that formed part of the blockade on February 17, 1864 in Charleston Harbor. Although the Hunley later sank, it was a major step towards submarine development and use. Later on, in World Wars I and II, submarines would play a major role in the fighting.

As we can see, the Civil War was unique in many ways. The tactics, wars, and technology all set new standards of how battles would be won and lost during the next 100 years.

Chapter 4: What was it like to be a kid during the American Civil War?

Have a look at the picture of a Civil War drummer below. How old do you think he was?

The boy in the picture is eleven years old. His name is Johnny Clem, and he was born in Ohio. When the Army wouldn't accept him as a soldier because he was too young, he enlisted as a drummer boy. For two years and during five major battles, Johnny marched alongside the Union soldiers in his regiment, banging on his little drum to keep them walking together. What do you think it would have been like to have gone with Johnny?

> **Did you know?**
>
> The Spencer repeating rifle could fire 14-20 rounds per minute. Muskets could only fire 2 or 3 rounds per minute

The first thing that we would have noticed would have been how long it took to get to the actual battles. Although the trains were used by the army, they were mainly used for taking supplies and large, heavy weapons to the battlefields. Most of the ordinary soldiers just had to walk to get to where they were going. Johnny walked and walked and walked.

When he finally got to the battlefield, he was not allowed to fight. Kids were too young to be carrying heavy weapons and to be running into enemy gunfire. Instead, kids were used as messengers. They were supposed to be ready at any time to take important messages from one general to another. Sometimes, the kids couldn't even go to sleep - just in case the general needed them. It wasn't always an easy life.

Do you think it would have been hard to be away from your family for two years? Although Johnny returned home to see his family, a lot of the men who marched with him on the 22nd Michigan Volunteer Infantry Regiment did not. In fact, of their group of 997 soldiers that left to fight, 399 of them died from battle wounds or disease. Can you imagine what it would have been like to see all that death? Would you have felt sad?

Being a kid during the Civil War meant helping the adults who were fighting. Whether banging a drum while they marched carrying messages, or taking care of the house while the fathers and brothers were away, the Civil War let everyone who wanted to be a part of it do so.

Chapter 5: How did the American Civil War end?

After the Battle of Gettysburg had been fought, the Union army began to push the retreating Confederates back into the South. The Union won victory after victory, and they practiced "total war" against the rebels. On April 9, 1865, after one last battle against the Union, Confederate General Robert E. Lee surrendered to Union forces. Part of the surrendering documents signed made sure that no soldiers would be punished for their roles in the war. Robert E. Lee himself went on to be an active figure in politics.

Most of the soldiers went back to try and rebuild the lives that they had left four years before. They went back to their jobs, and families that had lost sons, husbands, and brothers tried to continue on the best they could.

At first, many Southern soldiers did not want to accept the fact that they had lost the war. Even once the surrender documents were signed, many kept saying "the South will rise again", which meant that another rebellion could happen at any moment. In the years that followed, Robert E. Lee, Jefferson Davos, and other tried to help the Southerners see that the most important thing now was to support the Union and the new way of life. There was no point in trying to make things be like they had been before.

Chapter 6: What happened after the American Civil War?

As we have already seen, the American Civil War was a unique war in many ways. It greatly affected the way that nations would fight during next one hundred years. Repeating rifles, submarines, improved communication, trenches, and so on all became important parts of modern warfare. Even today, soldiers study the battles of the Civil War to learn how to fight nowadays. The men who fought on those battlefields became legends. No matter which side they supported (the South or the North) these soldiers and generals earned the respect of all Americans.

Because of the economic warfare waged by the North, the Federal government saw the need to help the Southern states to recover. From the end of the Civil War to 1877, the Federal government used heavy military presence and laws to rebuild the South and to make sure that the slaves freed under the thirteenth amendment were equal to the white citizens. Although the intentions were good, the Southern economy didn't recover until much later, and African Americans living in the South were not truly equal until the Civil Rights movements of the 1960s.

Little by little, Southern politicians became more active in national politics. They began to run for office, vote in elections, and to make their voice heard again. Northern politicians welcomed them back. Although they didn't agree with everything that was said, they knew that Southerners were Americans whose voices should be listened to.

However, not everyone was ready to become a united union again. There were some who were convinced that strong action was still necessary, and that the enemy soldiers should be punished for their actions. One such man was John Wilkes Booth, a famous actor of the day.

A Confederate sympathizer, John Wilkes Booth could not accept the defeat of the South that he loved so much. Together with a large group of people who thought like he did, he made a plan to kidnap several important Union politicians, including President Lincoln. However, once the South surrendered, Booth decided that revenge was a better plan. On April 14, 1865, just five days after the South surrendered, Booth shot Lincoln in the head at a theater and killed him. Lincoln had won the Civil War, but he was still ended up being one of its victims.

As the years went by, the nation began to feel united again. The wounds of war healed, the soldiers went home, and life went on.

Conclusion

The Civil War was a truly dark time in the history of the United States. It was a time when people thought more about their own problems and their own desires instead of what was good for the country as a whole. Families and friendships were destroyed, and many people died. In all, over a half a million soldiers died, and another 400,000 were wounded. There was not one family that did not lose somebody or that knew someone who died. Although there were some good results, like the end of slavery, it was a truly high price to pay.

Since that time, states across the country have built monuments and museums to teach the next generations about what happened during those four years. Have you ever been to visit some of the battlegrounds from the Civil War? You can see where the Battle of Gettysburg was fought, and where the Hunley sunk a Union ship. You can retrace the steps of Johnny Clem and the 22nd Michigan Volunteer Infantry Regiment as they fought their way across the Midwest and down into the South. You can see where Robert E. Lee surrendered, and where Lincoln was shot.

The Civil War may have happened a long time ago, but it still affects us today. We now know the importance of sticking together and talking out our differences. We learned that humans shouldn't be treated like property, but as people. We have also learned that, even in difficult times, we should always be brave and stand up for what is right.

The American Civil War was a time when everybody had to decide what they believed and to be ready to help others do the same. Have you learned the lesson?

Work Cited

IMAGES:

Currier and Ives: The battle of Gettysburg, Pa. July 3d. 1863. Hand-colored lithograph. Wikipedia.com. 26 January, 2005. 11 September 2012.

<http://en.wikipedia.org/wiki/Battle_of_Gettysburg>.

Whitney cotton gin, courtroom model, 1800. Photo. AmericanEnterprise.com. 12 September, 2012.

<http://americanenterprise.si.edu/portfolio/whitney-cotton-gin-courtroom-model-1800/>.

Portrait of Abraham Lincoln. Photo. Wikipedia.com. 11 December, 2011. 12 September, 2012.

< http://en.wikipedia.org/wiki/Abraham_Lincoln>.

Portrait of Jefferson Davis. Photo. Wikipedia.com. 26 December, 2009. 14 September, 2012.

<http://en.wikipedia.org/wiki/Jefferson_Davis>.

Schultze, Louis: Dred Scott. Painting. Wikipedia.com. 25 March, 2012. 13 September, 2012.

< http://en.wikipedia.org/wiki/Dred_Scott_v._Sandford>

Public Domain. Photo of Confederate money. Schmoop.com. 13 September, 2012.

< http://www.shmoop.com/civil-war/photo-confederate-money.html>.

Public Domain. Picture of African-American soldiers. Newsone.com. 31 May, 2011. 13 September, 2012.

< http://newsone.com/1270435/cleveland-remembers-black-civil-war-veterans/>.

Portrait of Johnny Clem. Photo. Civilwarsources.blogspot.com. 7 November, 2009. 13 September, 2012.

<http://civilwarsources.blogspot.com/2009/11/johnnie-clem-drummer-boy-of-shiloh.html>.

QUOTATIONS:

Lincoln, Abraham. Inaugural addresses of the presidents of the United States: from George Washington to George W. Bush. Bartleby.com. October 1993. 12 September 2012.

< http://www.bartleby.com/124/pres31.html>.

Lincoln, Abraham. Speech at New Haven. Historyplace.com. 13 September, 2012.

< http://www.historyplace.com/lincoln/haven.htm>.

Hammond, James Henry. On the Admission of Kansas, Under the Lecompton Constitution.

Sewanee.edu. 13 September 2012.

< http://www.sewanee.edu/faculty/willis/Civil_War/documents/HammondCotton.html>.

Made in the USA
San Bernardino, CA
23 February 2016